*Fortune knocks but once;
misfortune has much more patience.*

Jonathan Swift

---

he operating environment of every nonprofit organization is fraught with dangers. To ensure an organization's success, a board of directors or trustees must consciously face those risks and reduce them to a tolerable level. Because contemplating losses is not especially pleasurable, a well-meaning board may understandably, but unforgivably, neglect its duty. For many board members, awareness of risk remains in the shadowy realm beyond conscious thought as they focus on what their organizations can achieve if everything goes well. The purpose of this booklet is to shine some light into the darkness of loss and to provide boards with techniques for protecting their organizations and themselves from unanticipated losses.

Many risks are abundantly evident. We all recognize the risk that fire can destroy an organization's capacity to operate even if the organization rents space in a building with a fire alarm and sprinklers. At the worst, property losses of this sort are limited to the value of the organization's assets. Liability risks, on the other hand, may result in damage well beyond an organization's resources. With the decline of charitable immunity (the legal doctrine that at one time protected charitable organizations from financial responsibility for causing harm), legal liability for most nonprofit organizations is the same as it is for business firms. The nonprofit board itself may be exposed to risks equal to that of other corporate boards, or it may be protected somewhat by special state laws that will be discussed below. As the risk associated with nonprofits' legal liability has increased, managing that risk by purchasing liability insurance has become both more difficult and more expensive.

Liability risks are difficult to manage because they exist in such variety and may entail costs even if the organization has not caused any harm. Recently, the Boy Scouts of America and a local troop were sued for negligence in failing to protect a Scout from being molested by a Scoutmaster. The Scout sought punitive damages of $30 million. Although the national organization was absolved of liability, the local chapter was required to pay $45,000 in compensatory damages, and the national organization incurred substantial legal fees.

Any organization may face at some point the possibility of suit by a fired executive. Board members may be named directly in such an action and may need to pay an attorney even though they eventually prevail on the merits. Risks such as these, which imperil both the organization and the personal finances of directors and officers, require special risk-management strategies.

As the preceding examples illustrate, liability arising from risks from operation of even the smallest nonprofit organization can be enormous. Moreover, although it is readily apparent that nonprofit organizations face potential loss from the defense and payment of liability claims, in some situations the organization's board members, employees, or volunteers may also face liability. Moreover, the nonprofit organization may have insubstantial assets and, as a consequence, the involved individuals may have the only "deep pockets." Risk management provides techniques for controlling these perils.

The board's obligation is to ensure that risk management is an integral part of all organization activities. The board must play the lead and perform many risk-management functions itself. Boards of large organizations may be able to afford the services of a professional risk manager, and others may rely upon the organization's administrators to implement risk-management policies, but responsibility always lies with the board. Most boards would do well to have a risk-management committee with special, although hardly exclusive, responsibility for assessing and responding to risks. Developing a written risk-management policy is another effective means of demonstrating to insurers and staff that the board takes risk management very seriously.

FUNDAMENTALS OF RISK MANAGEMENT

Fortunately, the fundamentals of risk management that every nonprofit organization board member needs to understand are quite straight-forward and, for the most part, intuitively familiar. This booklet provides a means of approaching risk management systematically and brings to light some aspects of the process that might be overlooked. Before turning to the mechanics of the risk-management process, however, it is important to understand its goals.

Risk management is not the same as purchasing insurance, nor is the board's job limited to protecting its members from personal liability. Deciding whether to purchase insurance and, if so, how to obtain the best insurance value is an essential part of risk management, but it is far from the whole story. The primary goal of risk management is to enable the organization to survive and carry out its mission. Beyond survival, the goals of risk management vary depending on the purposes and objectives of individuals and organizations. Possible goals might include:

♦ Ensuring a safe environment for employees, volunteers, and service recipients;

♦ Reducing the anxiety and fear of liability of employees and volunteers;

♦ Conserving the assets of the organization so that it can pursue its mission;

♦ Ensuring compliance with legal requirements; and

♦ Ensuring that individuals harmed by the organization's activities receive adequate compensation.

Some of these goals can be achieved by purchasing insurance; some cannot. The most insurance can do is provide funds to pay for harm the organization causes. Preventing the harm is better than relying on insurance to pay a loss. Thus, a comprehensive risk-management program must transcend preoccupation with insurance.

THE BOARD'S SPECIAL RESPONSIBILITY FOR RISK MANAGEMENT

The board of directors bears responsibility for its organization's survival. To fulfill this responsibility, a board has a legal duty to conserve and protect the assets of the organization. These assets include not only money, property, and lives, but the goodwill and integrity of the organization as well. Through inaction or imprudence, the board itself may imperil the organization or impede it from achieving its goals. More positively, the board has the power to protect the organization from potential losses by attending to the risk-management implications of the following standard board functions:

- Establishing goals;
- Monitoring management;
- Ensuring the availability and proper use of funds; and
- Making necessary changes and monitoring the impact of changes.

Board members are generally responsible for exercising their corporate powers with the same skill and care as an ordinarily prudent person in the same circumstances. Additionally, directors must act in the organization's best interests rather than to achieve personal advantage. Failure to act prudently may expose a director to personal liability. Misconduct or imprudence also may result in the destruction or crippling of a much needed organization. To prevent the untimely demise of a nonprofit organization, risk management is essential. For the most part, good board procedures are themselves good risk-management procedures.

THE RISK-MANAGEMENT PROCESS

The structure of the risk-management process closely parallels any other exercise of effective management. The following five risk-management steps can be integrated into any organization's ongoing procedures:

Step 1: Identify risks;

Step 2: Analyze options for eliminating or reducing risks;

Step 3: Select the most suitable techniques;

Step 4: Implement the techniques; and

Step 5: Monitor the techniques and modify as needed.

STEP 1. IDENTIFY RISKS

The process of risk identification resembles a needs assessment. What does the organization do that might cause a loss, and what property does the organization control that might be lost or cause a loss? As with a needs assessment, risk identification methods differ among organizations, but they are always directed to the same questions.

A starting point for identifying risks, especially for older and larger organizations, is to review insurance claims histories. Examining claims histories alone, however, will not adequately identify risks and may foster overconfidence. Risks often exist despite the absence of claims. No one may have tripped on one of the throw rugs—yet. An organization that has never faced a liability claim may not sufficiently appreciate the effect a claim can have. Almost all losses occur with very low frequency, but when they occur, they may entail massive judgments and, even if the defendant organization prevails, result in costly legal fees and loss of staff time.

Because of the danger of overlooking risks and underestimating expected losses, claims histories are not adequate predictors of the future risk exposure. More useful are check lists and flow charts that are specific to an organization's anticipated activities. To develop an effective check list or flow chart, a nonprofit may wish to consult with its insurer, insurance broker, attorney, or a professional risk manager. Alternatively or in addition, a risk-management handbook may point out risks that do not immediately come to mind. Here are some common risks that are not readily recognized:

- Employees claiming wrongful termination or violation of their rights;
- Governmental entities claiming waste of assets, violation of reporting laws, or self-dealing;
- Environmental damage from toxic waste on property an organization acquires;
- Theft or destruction of materials that are worth far more to the organization than their insurable replacement value;
- Service recipients claiming negligent supervision or improper selection of employees and volunteers; and
- Violation of regulations governing the services the organization provides.

Because risks constantly change, the identification step must be repeated periodically. Moreover, to be most effective, risk identification must be integrated into everything the board and its organization do, and not considered only in relation to insurance. For example, the board of a San Francisco agency approved a lease without an escape clause in the event the leased property was damaged by an earthquake. Following the big quake in 1989, the organization faced the wholly unnecessary loss of paying rent for unusable space. Had the board been more conscious of the risk, it might have avoided the loss.

STEP 2. ANALYZE RISKS

In analyzing a risk, the expected loss is the most important value. Expected losses are calculated by multiplying expected claims frequency by expected claims severity. For example, an organization operating in a high crime area may anticipate an average of three thefts annually with an average loss of $200. Can the organization afford the $600 expected loss? Even if it can, does it need insurance in case losses are higher than expected? The hardest losses to estimate are the ones that occur with a low frequency but high severity. As the bumper sticker says, "One Nuclear Bomb Can Ruin Your Whole Day." Proper procedures at a nursing home can minimize the risk of contagious disease, but if a lethal epidemic breaks out, the organization must be prepared to respond to a financial burden far exceeding its annual budget. If the nursing home is to survive, its board must prepare for the possibility of such an epidemic.

Analysis of a risk should include specification of what makes the activity or item risky. A board can choose sensibly about how to deal with the risk only if it is aware of the risk elements. That information will be essential for deciding whether the risk can be reduced to an acceptable level or should be protected against in some fashion.

STEP 3. SELECT SUITABLE TECHNIQUES TO CONTROL RISKS

After analyzing a risk, the board must choose from among a variety of risk-management techniques that afford tremendous flexibility for responding in the manner most suitable for the organization's mission and resources. Each of the following techniques is discussed briefly below:

A. Avoidance;
B. Loss Control;
C. Separation;

D. Combination;

E. Retention; and

F. Transfer.

All risk-management techniques have advantages and disadvantages. Moreover, with the exception of avoidance, the techniques are not mutually exclusive. The best approach to managing risk will ordinarily be a combination of these techniques.

A. Avoidance

Avoidance eliminates the source of a risk. For example, some elementary schools fence their playgrounds and keep the gates locked after hours both to protect the facilities from damage and to avoid responsibility for accidents. A board may exercise avoidance by discontinuing a program or declining to expand the organization into new areas, but ordinarily *a board cannot avoid a risk merely by inaction.* Failure to address a risk may itself expose the board to liability.

Because avoidance means forgoing some activity, it is rarely the preferred risk-management option, but it may be necessary if other techniques cannot reduce risk to an acceptable level.

B. Loss Control (Risk Reduction)

Loss control reduces expected losses by decreasing the frequency and severity of risks. Responding to the risk of child abuse and of suits alleging that the organization does not adequately protect children in its program from pedophiles, some youth-serving organizations will not place a volunteer in the field without first checking police records. Adhering to this procedure decreases the likelihood of a child being molested, and if a child is molested, increases the probability that the organization will be able to defend successfully against a lawsuit.

A more common example of loss control is provided by the museum director who routinely walks through the entire facility to check for anything that might create a hazard for the public. Upon finding a hazard, she may remove it, post an adequate warning, or route the public away from it.

Many activities undertaken to increase organizational effectiveness also have the effect of reducing risks. Staff training undertaken to improve job performance generally will help staff members to avoid accidents and respond appropriately to other sources of loss. Performance training and risk-management training, however, are not synonymous. When training is designed to increase efficiency or reduce costs rather than to improve quality, one unintended side effect may be to increase risks. By encouraging management to be sensitive to the loss control implications of every undertaking, the board can ensure an appropriate balance of risk and efficiency.

C. Separation

Separation is best exemplified by the adage, "Don't put all your eggs in one basket." Separation may be especially useful for reducing losses of irreplaceable items, such as donor lists. One list could be kept in the office and the other could be stored at an executive officer's home or in a safe deposit box. The same arrangement is strongly recommended for all important computer files and software.

Separation may also be valuable for managing liability risks. A multi-faceted nonprofit organization might establish one corporate entity to run a community theater and another to operate a homeless shelter. Once the assets of the parent corporation are separated into two distinct legal entities, a claim against one ordinarily does not jeopardize assets of the other. Separately incorporating a commercial enterprise may be the best way to insulate the host organization from the liability risks involved in running a business.

D. Combination (Diversification)

The philosophy behind combination is that big is better—especially if growth is accompanied by diversification. One organization with a large number of different types of risk is better positioned to manage them than are several small organizations, each subject mainly to one type of risk. Although this idea may seem counterintuitive, it has a sound basis in probability theory. The greater the variety of risks, the lower the likelihood that they will all materialize simultaneously. With larger numbers of more diverse risks, actual losses tend more closely to approximate expected losses, which makes prospective financing much easier.

Although combination may be inadvisable for any particular organization, it might prove very useful for a group of organizations that can combine their risks. A number of options for group insurance purchasing and risk pooling discussed below enable organizations to do that. Insurance itself operates on the principle that losses are manageable if shared among a sufficiently large group.

E. Retention

Retention is a strategic decision to bear a risk. For example, a community center may have a twenty-year-old station wagon that it uses for running errands and transporting volunteers. Despite its great sentimental value and utility to the center, the car is worth only $500. Instead of purchasing collision insurance to guard against the risk of damage, the center could retain the risk of collision loss. Consequently, if the auto is damaged in an accident, the center would bear a $500 loss. With a more expensive vehicle, the center might choose an insurance policy that has a $500 deductible. Strategic retention of small risks can substantially reduce insurance costs because small losses are relatively expensive to insure.

F. Transfer

Finally, an organization may transfer a risk to another party. Risk may be transferred by insurance or by contract. By contract, an organization may agree to provide services for a municipality provided that the government hold the organization harmless, i.e., the city will pay claims filed against the organization for harm occurring in the course of providing the contracted service. Insurance is the more typical method of transferring a risk.

Transfer may be partial or complete. The transfer of risk by insurance is always partial. At most, the financial consequences of the risk are transferred. Using the preceding example, the community center could transfer the financial impact of liability associated with operating the station wagon by purchasing auto liability insurance. Or, the center could transfer all the risks associated with the station wagon by selling it and contracting with a taxi company to meet its transportation needs.

(Unlike the risks involved in transportation, the board cannot transfer the risks of governance by delegating its responsibility to guide the organization and to look after its welfare. The board can, however, transfer some of the risk of financial loss for its actions. Indemnification and insurance for directors and officers are discussed in more detail toward the end of this booklet.)

STEP 4. IMPLEMENT SELECTED RISK-MANAGEMENT TECHNIQUES

After selecting appropriate risk-management techniques, the board must insist upon action to implement the decision. The importance of involving every individual in the organization, from the chief executive officer to the occasional volunteer, in implementation is even greater than for the other risk-management steps. An unpaid volunteer may be thought to cost nothing, until that volunteer causes an accident or other loss. Given the possibility that any person acting on behalf of the organization can jeopardize its existence, the board cannot allow anyone to be excluded from the implementation process.

Board support for risk management must be unequivocal if its message is to have the desired impact throughout the organization. Having expressed itself, the board must ensure that management accepts the letter and spirit of board's risk management policies and is committed to infusing risk management into the organization's daily operations.

STEP 5. MONITOR AND MODIFY THE RISK-MANAGEMENT PROGRAM

The final step in the risk-management process requires monitoring the selected techniques and modifying as needed. Nonprofit organizations do not operate in a vacuum. Legal standards constantly change in ways that affect both risks and the options for dealing with them. For example, some state laws protect volunteer board members from personal liability only if the organization itself carries insurance. Similarly, enhanced knowledge and technology may both pose new risks and create new techniques for improving the risk-management process. Only by monitoring the implementation of its chosen techniques and periodically repeating the other steps of the risk-management process can an organization adequately reduce the danger of unpleasant surprises.

THE STRATEGIC USE OF INSURANCE

If a risk cannot be eliminated or reduced to an acceptable level, insurance becomes very attractive. Ideally, an organization could purchase an "all-risk" insurance policy and meet its insurance needs in a single move. "Package policies" from some insurance companies approximate this ideal, but do not cover all risks. Most organizations can obtain comprehensive insurance coverage only by piecing together several policies because insurers classify risks in discrete categories and offer specialized policies to tailor coverage depending on the particular risks of the policyholder. (See list of categories on page 17.) Because individual policies for each of these types of coverage differ somewhat among insurers, special care is needed to avoid either gaps or overlaps in the complete coverage package. Gaps can also occur when changing insurers, especially if either the old or new policy is written on a claims-made basis (see next section). The assistance of an insurance broker or other advisor can be invaluable in coordinating policies. A lawyer might also be helpful, but few lawyers are insurance experts.

INSURANCE PURCHASING

The need to understand risk and protect against loss might account for the popularity of insurance agents and brokers on nonprofit organization boards. Their expertise can be of tremendous value in evaluating insurance alternatives, but using their professional services may seriously disadvantage the organization. Because nonprofits constitute a small segment of the insurance market, insurance professionals who do not specialize in serving nonprofits may be unaware of special insurance options for nonprofits. Because some insurance companies limit who can sell their policies, an agent on the board may lack authority to obtain the best policy.

Whoever assumes the responsibility of obtaining insurance has the challenge of obtaining suitable coverage initially and of notifying the insurer thereafter of material changes in the organization's circumstances. In this process, the objective is to convince the insurer that the organization is as good a risk as its circumstances warrant. The lack of familiarity of most insurance professionals with nonprofit organizations suggests the desirability of dealing with an agent or broker who specializes in providing coverage for nonprofits.

Soliciting competitive bids is generally advisable, provided that the comparison process goes beyond price. Selecting the policy with the lowest premium may be the worst bargain an organization ever makes. Ordinarily when an organization buys something, the most the organization stands to lose is the purchase price. With insurance, the organization may lose the total amount of the coverage. Is a $1,000 saving worth a $1 million risk? The scope of the coverage and the integrity of the insurer are much more important factors than price.

Assessing the scope of coverage necessitates *reading the policy* — an agent's oral representations often cannot be enforced. The likelihood of being able to comprehend policy language has risen in recent years with the advent of plain English policy forms. Comprehension may be aided by knowing that insurance policies are written to give with one hand and take away with another. The insurance clause, the giving hand, is usually very inclusive. "This policy covers all . . ." Much of what the insurance clause gives, the policy's definitions and exclusions may take away. Is a volunteer an "employee"? Does the exclusion of pollution damage apply to a leaky septic tank?

Whether insurance is written on an "occurrence" or "claims-made" basis also substantially affects the scope of coverage. Until recently, the occurrence policy form had been standard for almost all insurance. With occurrence coverage, an incident is covered if it occurs within the policy period. Coverage under a claims-made policy depends on when a claim is filed. If an incident occurs during the policy period, but a claim is not filed until after a specified later date, the claim may not be honored. The occurrence form is generally preferable, but not always available.

In obtaining insurance, an organization need not venture alone into a world dominated by for-profit businesses. Numerous national and state associations offer sponsored programs or group purchasing arrangements that are tailored to the needs of nonprofit organizations. Besides generally offering more appropriate policy forms, these group programs may reduce the policyholders' insurance costs. If loss experiences for the group are favorable, the members may receive lower premiums, expanded coverage, or other improvements that would not be available to an organization acting alone. Participating in such a program may also improve the likelihood that coverage will continue, although no arrangement can guarantee insurance availability under all conditions.

In some states, nonprofit organizations have joined together to create their own insurance pools. Nonprofits in states without such arrangements may wish to draw upon the experience of the operational pools to create new ones, which are authorized under some state laws and the federal Risk Retention Act, which permits organizations to form a special type of liability insurance company.

Insurance pools and risk-retention groups function like insurance companies, but are subject to less regulation in the states where they do business. The principal feature that distinguishes them from commercial insurance companies is that they are owned by, and are hence responsible to, their member policyholders. If the members have few losses, the financial benefits redound to them. Within limits, members of a pool or risk-retention group can reduce the severity of the violent swings in availability and price common to the standard insurance market.

These insurance alternatives are not without risks and drawbacks of their own. Forming an insurance pool or risk-retention group may not be either feasible or advisable. The decision to join an existing operation should be made only after careful consideration because these alternatives are subject to less exacting scrutiny by regulatory authorities.

DIRECTORS AND OFFICERS

The protection of directors and officers presents a special problem because their activities and perhaps their personal resources may make them attractive litigation targets. The personal liability of directors and officers differs substantially from state to state. The traditional rule has been that directors and officers are personally liable for a breach of their duties of care, loyalty, or obedience to the organization. In some states, this traditional rule has been changed by legislation that either reduces the standard of care, e.g., imposes liability only if harm results from intentional misconduct rather than from simple negligence, or provides a good faith defense. Although passed to protect the personal assets of directors and officers, some of these laws may not have that effect because they are badly drafted or unconstitutional. The best method of reducing the risk of a lawsuit is the prudent exercise of authority in meeting the responsibilities of leadership. Residual risks may be dealt with through indemnification or insurance.

The essence of indemnification is that an organization will use its resources to protect board members and officers from personal liability for actions undertaken within the scope of their duties. Through indemnification, a suit against an individual acting on behalf of an organization would result in the organization rather than the individual paying the defense costs and any settlement or judgment in favor of the claimant. Many states permit indemnification only as provided for in an organization's charter or bylaws.

The utility of indemnification is limited in several respects. First, most states do not allow indemnification unless the director prevails in defending a claim, and indemnification is improper in situations where a director breaches certain duties to the organization. Indemnifying an officer who misappropriated funds or otherwise benefitted at the organization's expense would be ludicrous. Personal liability for fines and punitive damages may not be indemnified because of the public interest in holding individuals responsible when they willfully violate established rules. Finally, indemnification is only as good as the source of funds earmarked to finance the indemnity. For an organization with few assets, indemnification may be of little or no value.

General liability policies cover some losses that directors and officers may cause. These policies typically pay if their action causes property damage or bodily injury to another party, and some offer even broader coverage. For harm resulting from executive decision-making, directors and officers insurance (D&O) or association professional liability insurance (APLI) is necessary. Association professional liability insurance provides the equivalent of D&O coverage for suits against directors and officers plus protection for the organization itself.

Directors and officers insurance provides two separate forms of coverage that dovetail with indemnification (and should be coordinated with the indemnification provisions in an organization's bylaws). The first form of coverage pertains to the personal liability of the directors and officers. Thus, D & O insurance may protect a director or officer even when indemnification would be impermissible. Additionally, the policy covers expenses that an organization may incur in the course of resolving a claim against its directors or officers.

Although D&O insurance provides substantial protection, coverage exclusions limit its utility as a risk-management tool. Directors and officers policies commonly exclude the following:

- Fines and penalties imposed by law;
- Libel and slander;
- Personal profit;
- Dishonesty;
- Failure to procure or maintain insurance;
- Claims arising under the Employee Retirement Income Security Act;
- Bodily injury and property damage claims;
- Pollution claims; and
- Suits by one board member against another.

Exactly what D&O insurance does cover depends on the terms of the particular policy. Directors and officers insurance policies are commonly written on a claims-made basis. Unlike most general liability policies, D&O policies usually do not provide for the insurer to defend against a claim. The organization or individual sued must first pay attorneys' fees and then seek reimbursement from the insurer. Terms of specific policies vary considerably, making further generalization impossible.

RISK-MANAGEMENT FRUSTRATIONS

Developing risk-management awareness may open the door to undiscovered opportunities, but it may also bring frustration when the most prudent choices are not available or the rewards are not immediately apparent. The principal benefit of risk management—reduced losses—may seem illusory, especially to the organization that has never been sued. Who can get excited because a bad thing that might have happened didn't happen or happened in a way that was not as bad as it could have been? Nevertheless, risk management is a critical part of board responsibilities.

One of the more tangible and immediate benefits of effective risk management can be lower insurance costs. Unfortunately, savings are likely to be less than one might reasonably expect. Although all insurance companies encourage risk management, they may not reward it with lower premiums. The hard fact is that nonprofit organizations represent a relatively small portion of the insurance market. Consequently, insurers are often unwilling to make substantial accommodations for nonprofit organizations, even those with stellar risk-management programs and claims histories.

Moreover, with the exception of insurers that specialize in nonprofits, underwriters often lack a full understanding of the nature of nonprofit operations. Consequently, underwriters may be unable to distinguish between an organization that is a proverbial accident waiting to happen and an organization that is unlikely to suffer a loss. Finally, insurers generally insist upon a minimum premium for writing a policy. Many small nonprofit organizations qualify for that minimum premium and therefore will not be charged a lower amount regardless of their extreme care and prudence. For most nonprofits, the principal effects of risk management on insurance will be to increase the likelihood that they can qualify for coverage and decrease the likelihood of cancellation.

CONCLUSION

A board active in risk management can help an organization achieve its maximum potential. The board can serve as a catalyst for recognizing opportunities at the same time it reduces the likelihood that an organization will suffer losses. For these reasons, boards of for-profit businesses have typically assigned a high priority to effective risk management. If nonprofit organizations are to fulfill their obligations to the communities they serve and the people who toil on their behalf, they need to make a similar commitment to identifying risks and keeping them under control.

RECOGNIZING AND RESPONDING TO RISKS
―――――――――――― ♦ ――――――――――

Listed on the following page are some of the common, but often unrecognized, risks of operating a nonprofit organization. For each, the board needs to respond by assessing how the risk can be best managed. Risk reduction through training and prudent conduct are generally the most effective strategies. Because insurance may also be needed to protect the organization and everyone associated with it from an irreducible risk of financial loss, this list identifies the type of insurance that will usually cover a particular risk.

Be aware, however, that policies differ. Types of insurance listed in the third column are broadly appropriate for the major sources of risk associated with the corresponding organizational component in the first column. In addition, coverage for many special risks may be included in a general liability policy or obtained most economically as an endorsement to a general liability policy. *This list should be used only as a general guideline for structuring the insurance component of a risk-management program.* To be certain that a risk is indeed insured, close examination of an insurance policy's terms is essential.

COMPONENT	SOURCES OF RISK	TYPE OF INSURANCE
Board	Self-dealing Tax Penalties Executive Decisions Regulations Fiduciary Duties	Directors & Officers (D&O) Association Professional Liability Insurance (APLI)

Services	Common Torts
	  (Negligence)
	Malpractice
		General Liability (GL)
		Errors and Omissions (E&O)
		Professional Liability
		  (Malpractice)

Employees*	Injury Wrongful Termination Civil Rights	Workers Compensation, D&O APLI, some GL policies
Volunteers*	Injury	Volunteer, APLI
Certification	Antitrust	APLI, E&O
Publications	Defamation	Publishers
Transportation	Accidents	Auto Non-owned auto
Money	Theft Embezzlement	Property Bond
Fundraising	Various	Specialty Coverages
Special Events	Product Liability	Completed Products

* Separate policies are required to protect against risks from and to employees and volunteers. The types of insurance listed for employees and volunteers pertain only to claims they may file against an organization. For example, a wrongful termination claim may be covered under either a D&O policy or a GL policy. Insurance for types of harm a volunteer may cause are listed for the type of activity in which they are engaged, e.g., fundraising.

SUGGESTED RESOURCES

Directors and Officers Liability Insurance and Indemnification. Washington, DC: Council on Foundations, 1989, 35 pages.

>An introduction to directors and officers insurance and indemnification, written in question and answer format. This publication is targeted to foundation executives, but almost all of its material is equally applicable to all nonprofit organization boards and officers.

Kurtz, Daniel L. *Board Liability: Guide for Nonprofit Directors.* Mt. Kisco, NY: Moyer Bell Ltd., 1988, 179 pages.

>A discussion of board members' obligations to their organizations and the exposures to liability that serving as a board member entails for both the individual and the organization. An explanation of insurance and indemnity issues for boards is included.

Lai, Mary L., Terry S. Chapman & Elmer L. Steinbock. *Am I Covered for...? A Guide to Insurance for Non-Profits.* San Jose, CA: Consortium for Human Services, 1992, 300 pages.

>This handbook on insurance purchasing for nonprofits includes checklists, worksheets, forms, and examples for use in evaluating the need for insurance and obtaining the best policies at the lowest cost.

State Liability Laws for Charitable Organizations and Volunteers. Washington, DC: National Center for Community Risk Management & Insurance, 1992, 48 pages.

>A state-by-state compilation of volunteer protection laws and limitations on the liability of charitable organizations. The book examines the scope, conditions, and limitations of more than 100 laws and court cases. Comparison tables highlight differences among states.

Tremper, Charles. *D & O...Yes or No? Directors and Officers Insurance for the Volunteer Board.* Washington, DC: National Center for Community Risk Management & Insurance, 1991, 20 pages.

>This booklet examines each of the major considerations in deciding whether to purchase directors and officers insurance and, if so, which policy to select.

Tremper, Charles. *Reconsidering Legal Liability and Insurance for Nonprofit Organizations.* Lincoln, NE: Law College Education Services, Inc., (distributed by the Society for Nonprofit Organizations, Madison, WI), 1989, 213 pages.

>A policy-oriented examination of the legal liability and insurance for nonprofit organizations. The book offers suggestions for managing risk within the existing legal and insurance structure as well as for changing the laws and creating more satisfactory insurance arrangements.

About the Authors

Charles Tremper is founding executive director of the Nonprofit Risk Management Center, which helps nonprofits to prevent injuries, comply with the law, and obtain adequate insurance at reasonable rates. Previously he taught at the National Law Center of George Washington University and the University of Nebraska College of Law. He has also been a visiting scholar at Yale University's Program on Non-Profit Organizations and a Bush Foundation fellow in child development and social policy.

George Babcock practices law in Omaha, Nebraska, and is an adjunct professor at the University of Nebraska's Omaha campus. A member of the Society of Chartered Property and Casualty Underwriters, he served as senior vice president of a surplus lines insurance brokerage and managing general agency. His experience includes a stint at Lloyd's of London.